INVENTING THE
PERSONAL COMPUTER

BY ANGIE SMIBERT

Published by The Child's World®
1980 Lookout Drive • Mankato, MN 56003-1705
800-599-READ • www.childsworld.com

Acknowledgments
The Child's World®: Mary Berendes, Publishing Director
Red Line Editorial: Design, editorial direction, and production
Photographs ©: Pornsak Paewlumfaek/Shutterstock Images, cover, 1; Bettmann/
Corbis, 4; ClassicStock/Corbis, 6; Karsten Lemm/DPA/Corbis, 8; J. Scott Applewhite/
AP Images, 10; Veronika Lukasova/ZumaPress/Corbis, 12; Doug Wilson/Corbis, 15;
DB Apple/DPA/Corbis, 16; Dennis Van Tine/LFI/Photoshot/Newscom, 19; Roger
Ressmeyer/Corbis, 20

ISBN 9781634074582

LCCN 2015946290

Printed in the United States of America
Mankato, MN
December, 2015
PA02284

ABOUT THE AUTHOR

Angie Smibert is the author of several young adult science fiction novels,
including the *Memento Nora* series. She has authored numerous short
stories and several educational titles. Angie was also a science writer and
Web developer at NASA's Kennedy Space Center for many years. She
received NASA's prestigious Silver Snoopy and several other awards for
her work.

TABLE OF
CONTENTS

Chapter 1

EARLY DAYS

It was 1956. A young engineer pressed his face against the plate-glass window. Behind it sat UNIVAC. The computer was 50 feet (15 m) long and as tall as a person. On its front, spools of **magnetic tape** whirred round and round. Lights blinked.

The young man was excited that his company now had "an electronic brain."[1] That's what the television commercials called the UNIVAC. It was one of the first computers that companies could buy. And it was a marvel. UNIVAC used **transistors**, which are small electronic devices made from **silicon**. They control the flow of electricity inside a computer. Their small size would change computers forever.

Only the experts in white lab coats could touch the UNIVAC. The engineer was disappointed that he was not allowed in the room. He had spent all morning typing instructions on a keypunch machine. It cut holes in stiff pieces of paper called punch cards. He handed his stack of punch cards to the expert, who fed them

◄ Workers operate a UNIVAC computer in the 1950s.

into the computer. The engineer could only wait as the big "brain" blinked and whirred.

While he waited, the engineer dreamed of having a computer of his very own. He certainly could not afford a UNIVAC or anything like it. In 1956, the company paid $4,000 a month just to rent the massive computer. The engineer could buy a luxury car for that much money! But the size and cost did not stop him from dreaming. He wanted a computer that he could build. He wanted one that he could program. He wanted one that might even sit on his desk.

The engineer read electronics magazines and tinkered with electronics kits in his garage. So did many other young people in the 1950s and 1960s. That's when the personal computer revolution began.

◀ The UNIVAC's control panel had many switches.

Chapter 2

MICROPROCESSORS

Ted Hoff was a fan of computers. In 1969, he worked for a new company called Intel. His boss asked him to design a chip for a Japanese calculator maker. Back in 1958, engineers had found that they could put many transistors on one sliver of silicon. This came to be called a chip.

Silicon chips became big business. The Japanese company wanted a chip that could calculate. At that time, most chips performed only one function or task. They turned electrical signals into numbers.

But Hoff wanted the chip to do more. So, he designed a chip that could actually run programs. His chip turned electrical signals into instructions that told the chip to do something. The Japanese company was not happy. They had just wanted a simple chip. But Intel decided to make the new chip anyway.

◄ The chip that Ted Hoff designed was about the size of a fingernail.

Hoff's new chip came out in 1971. It was called the Intel 4004. It was the first all-purpose chip. Intel called it a "computer on a chip."[2] This type of chip is called a **microprocessor**.

Intel went to work on designing faster and better microprocessors. By 1974, it had released the Intel 8008 and the more powerful 8080 microprocessors. Other companies were making microprocessors, too. But Intel's 8080 became the basis of many computer kits. These kits had many parts. People had to follow detailed instructions to build the computers. One of these kits was the famous Altair 8800.

◀ In 2010, Ted Hoff received a medal for inventing the first microprocessor.

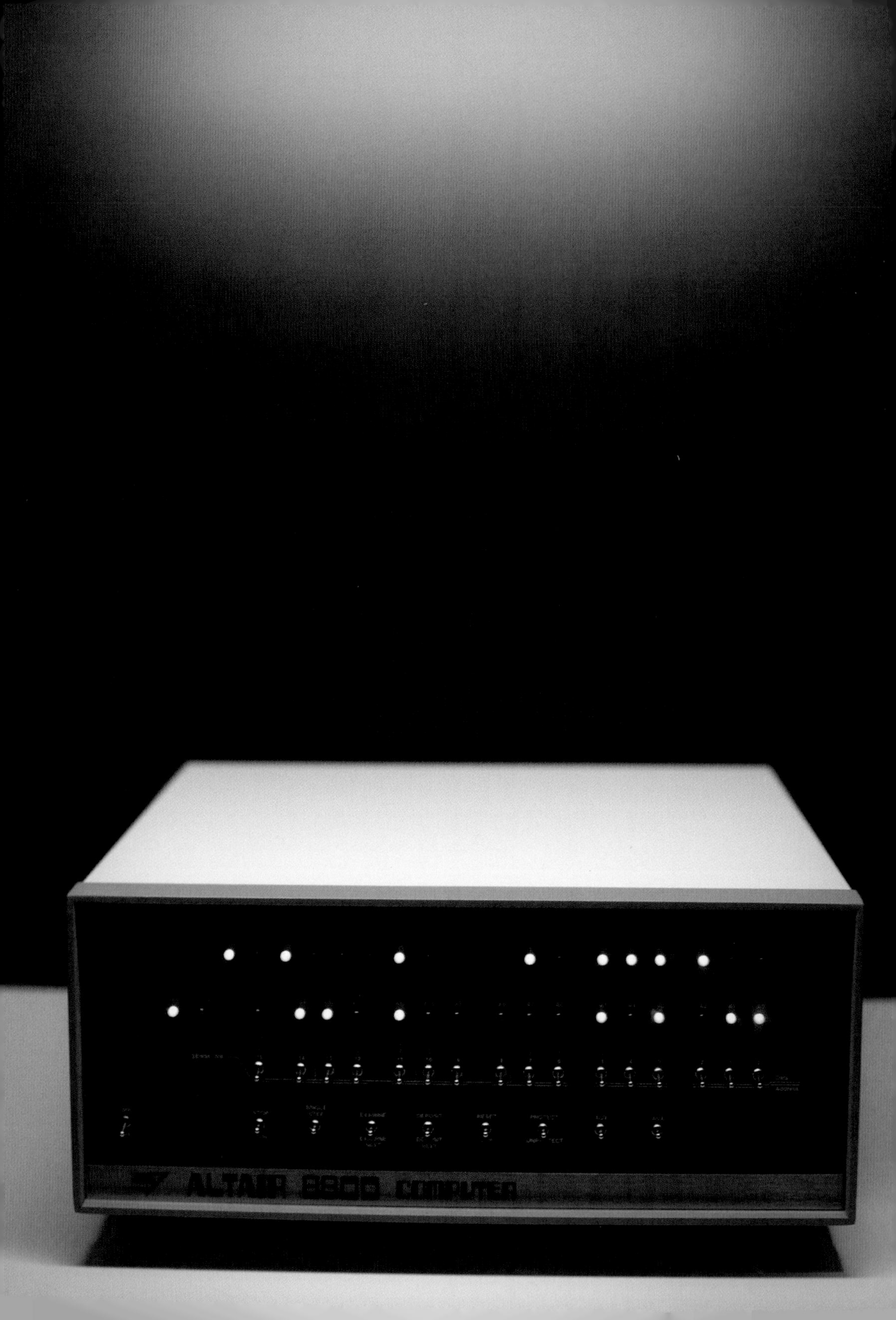
ALTAIR 8800 COMPUTER

Chapter 3

ALTAIR 8800

In 1974, Les Solomon was the editor of *Popular Electronics* magazine. His readers liked to put together electronic gadgets such as radios and metal detectors. Solomon thought readers would also like to build computers. So he contacted Ed Roberts. Roberts's company, MITS, made calculators. Solomon asked Roberts to design a computer kit that would sell for less than $500. In return, *Popular Electronics* would put the computer on its cover. Roberts knew this meant the kit would sell.

Roberts jumped at the chance. His company was failing. He thought the new kit might save MITS. His team designed a computer based on Intel's new 8080 microprocessor. They called the computer the Altair 8800.

Roberts shipped the computer to the magazine. Solomon needed to photograph the Altair 8800 for the cover. However, the package got lost in the mail. So the MITS team quickly put together an empty **casing** and sent it to the magazine. The

◀ The Altair 8800 did not have a monitor.

magazine's readers would not know the casing didn't have a computer inside!

The Altair 8800 appeared on the cover of the January 1975 issue of *Popular Electronics.* The magazine's readers ordered thousands of kits. Roberts's company was saved, and the Altair 8800 began a new age of computers.

The Altair 8800 did not actually do much on its own except blink. On the outside, it was a metal box with lights and switches. Inside, it had five computer boards. One of these had the Intel 8080 microprocessor on it. The owner could write his or her own programs and feed them into the box by flipping the switches on the front. This took a lot of work. Computer clubs sprang up across the country. Most tried to figure out what to do with the Altair 8800.

In 1975, two college students from Boston saw the Altair 8800. They saw it needed a better way to be programmed. These students called Roberts and offered to sell him a version of BASIC they had written. BASIC stands for Beginner's All-purpose Symbolic Instruction Code. It is a simple computer language that makes it easier for people to write programs.

These students were Bill Gates and Paul Allen. Roberts hired them to write software for the Altair 8800. Shortly after that, Gates and Allen started a company called Microsoft.

▲ Bill Gates (left) and Paul Allen (right) made Microsoft into one of the most successful companies in the world.

Chapter 4

APPLE

O n a cool, rainy day in March 1975, 30 members of the Homebrew Computer Club crowded into Gordon French's garage in Menlo Park, California. It was their first meeting. Most of the guys in the garage worked at local electronics companies. They liked to tinker with electronics at home, too. Now they had a club to swap ideas, plans, and even parts to make their own computers. This first meeting was all about the Altair 8800. French had the first one in the area.

Almost everyone in the garage was talking about the computer kit. But sitting near the back of the garage, a young engineer just listened. His name was Steve Wozniak. He was very shy. The club passed out a data sheet that explained how the microprocessor worked. Wozniak realized the Altair 8800 was very similar to a computer he had built five years earlier. The big difference was the chip. The Altair 8800 had a microprocessor. "It was as if my whole life had been leading up to this point," Wozniak later wrote. "That

◄ Steve Wozniak (left) and Steve Jobs (right) work on computers in a garage.

night . . . this whole vision of a personal computer popped into my head. All at once. Just like that."[3]

Wozniak saw how he could build the computer he had always wanted. All he needed was one of the new chips. That meeting inspired him to design one of the first true personal computers.

After that first meeting of the Homebrew Computer Club, Wozniak began building a computer. He wanted to show the club members they did not need a kit to make a computer. He also wanted his computer to be much more than the Altair 8800. Every computer up until then was just a box with lights and switches. Wozniak wanted one with a screen and keyboard. He wanted to be able to type words into the computer and have them show up on a screen. This had not been done before.

As he worked on it, Wozniak brought the new computer to every meeting of the Homebrew Computer Club and answered questions about it. The computer had the same number of chips the Altair 8800 had. But Wozniak's computer did so much more. It could even run a few games.

Wozniak also showed his design to his friend Steve Jobs. Jobs came to several Homebrew meetings with Wozniak. Jobs realized that many people might not be able to make the computer themselves. He suggested building and selling the computer already assembled.

So Jobs and Wozniak started their own company. To get money for it, Jobs sold his van. Wozniak sold an expensive calculator. After Jobs returned from visiting an apple orchard, he suggested a name for the company: Apple. Jobs and Wozniak founded Apple in 1976. Their first computer was called the Apple I.

Their first order came from a local computer store. The owner was also a member of the Homebrew club. He had seen the computer in action. He wanted to buy dozens of them for $500 each. Then he would sell them in his store for $666 each.

Jobs and Wozniak scrambled to build the Apple I computers. They paid friends to help assemble the computers in Jobs's garage. They built about 200 computers. Within a year, they had sold nearly all of them.

Wozniak soon began working on the Apple II. For this one, he wanted graphics, sounds, and even games. This meant designing a whole new computer.

Jobs dreamed big, too. He wanted the Apple II to be a computer everyone might use. The new computer needed to be sold as a complete package. The Apple I did not come with a keyboard or even a casing. So, the Apple II needed a keyboard and a great casing. Up until then, most computers were ugly gray metal boxes. Jobs had the Apple II covered in a sleek plastic casing. The keyboard and computer were one piece. The Apple II first appeared at the West Coast Computer Faire in April 1977. The computer was a huge success.

In the next few years, many companies began making their own personal computers. Five years after the Altair 8800 was on the cover of *Popular Electronics*, the personal computer was a billion-dollar business. This rapid growth continued for many years. By 2015, more than 80 percent of American households had at least one personal computer.

COMPUTER TIMELINE

1951	UNIVAC, the first commercial computer, is built.
1971	The first microprocessor, the Intel 4004, is invented.
1975	The Altair 8800 appears on the cover of *Popular Electronics*.
1976	Apple is founded, and the Apple I is released.
1977	Apple II becomes the first true personal computer.
2015	Eight of ten American homes have a personal computer.

GLOSSARY

casing (KAY-sing): A casing is a hard, protective cover. Many small pieces of electronic equipment are inside a computer's casing.

magnetic tape (mayg-NET-ik TAYP): Magnetic tape is a tape used to record sound, pictures, and computer data. The computer saved the results on magnetic tape.

microprocessor (MYK-roh-PRAH-ses-er): A microprocessor is a device in a computer that manages information and controls what the computer does. A computer with a fast microprocessor can play videos.

program (PRO-gram): Program means to give a set of instructions to a computer so that it does something useful. When people program computers, they can create things such as games.

silicon (SIL-i-kon): Silicon is a chemical element found in Earth's crust. Most computer chips are made of silicon.

software (SOFT-wair): Software is a computer program that helps users do certain tasks. Some software is for writing, some is for using the Web, and some is for playing games.

transistors (tran-ZIS-terz): Transistors are small devices used to control the flow of electricity. The invention of transistors made it possible for computers, radios, and other electronics to be made smaller.

TO LEARN MORE

Books

Gregory, Josh. *Steve Jobs*. New York: Children's Press, 2013.

Groves, Marsha. *Inventing the Computer*. New York: Crabtree, 2007.

Ventura, Marne. *The 12 Biggest Breakthroughs in Computer Technology*. North Mankato, MN: Peterson, 2015.

Web Sites

Visit our Web site for links about personal computers:
childsworld.com/links

Note to Parents, Teachers, and Librarians: We routinely verify our Web links to make sure they are safe and active sites. So encourage your readers to check them out!

SOURCE NOTES

1. "Fifties Advertising: UNIVAC Computer Commercial (5 February 1956) (Ad 2 of 2)." *Internet Archive*. Internet Archive, n.d. Web. 12 Aug. 2015.

2. Martin Campbell-Kelly, William Aspray, Nathan Ensmenger, and Jeffrey R. Yost. *Computer: A History of the Information Machine*. Boulder, CO: Westview, 2014. Print. 210.

3. Steve Wozniak and Gina Smith. *iWoz: Computer Geek to Cult Icon: How I Invented the Personal Computer, Co-founded Apple, and Had Fun Doing It*. New York: Norton, 2006. Print. 155–156.

INDEX